Live it up

Priceless secrets to your best life

POONAM KALRA

Worldwide Publishing by

Pendown Press

Powered by  Gullybaba

PENDOWN PRESS
Powered by **Gullybaba Publishing House Pvt. Ltd.,**
An ISO 9001 & ISO 14001 Certified Co.,
Regd. Office: 2525/193, 1st Floor, Onkar Nagar-A, Tri Nagar,
Delhi-110035
Ph.: 09350849407, 09312235086
E-mail: info@pendownpress.com
Branch Office: 1A/2A, 20, Hari Sadan, Ansari Road,
Daryaganj, New Delhi–110002
Ph.: 011-45794768
Website: PendownPress.com

First Edition: 2021

ISBN: 978-93-5554-106-2

Layout and Cover Designed by Pendown Graphics Team
Printed and Bound in India by Thomson Press India Ltd.

CONTENTS

Acknowledgement

This book and everything else in life wouldn't have been possible without the love, support and encouragement of my husband, Baldev Raj Kalra. Thank you for always being the anchor of my life.

Special thanks to my children Ashu Kadakia, Shubee Sikka & Amit Kalra. You are the reason for my being. I am so proud of you all, and your happiness multiplies mine.

Also, big thanks to my sons-in-law Vishal Kadakia & Sandeep Sikka and my daughter-in-law Poonam A Kalra. All three of you have made life even sweeter.

And then two more special people made my dream of writing a book come true.

First, Neetu Singhal, Chief Editor Navdrishti Times Newspaper & Magazine who introduced me to Dinesh Verma, CEO of Pendown Press, on hearing about my desire. Thank you, Neetu, for helping me take the first step toward writing my book.

Huge thanks to Dinesh Verma, my writing mentor and book strategist and the entire Pendown team for making the journey from an idea to a published author smooth and stress-free.

SECTION 1

HEALTH IS YOUR REAL WEALTH; CLAIM IT IMMEDIATELY!

Chapter 1

From My Heart To Yours

Hello friends, friends I am Poonam Kalra.

Life is a blessing that I have never taken for granted, and I never want any of my wonderful friends to take it for granted either.

At Seventy blessed years of life, I stand tall, happy, prosperous, showered by love and surrounded by loved ones, and I sincerely wish the same for you all.

With the grace of the almighty, my belief in myself and most importantly, the support of my progressive and loving husband, I have created for myself and my family the life that I always dreamed of.

The path was challenging as anything worthwhile is, but I never backed down from a challenge all my life.

For a shy newlywed, shifting to Delhi from Lucknow was not an easy transition. However, my husband was the wind beneath my wings and my anchor at sea who helped me soar into the sky to live my dreams and swim against the tide whenever any challenges arose.

Throughout my life, I have always lived with hope in my heart, Joy in my being and the warmth of the sun in my smile.

I have always shared my love, prosperity and wisdom freely and with an open heart.

With the advent of the Pandemic, humanity faced a challenge like never before, and the need for sharing hope and love and connecting to people was more important than ever.

The love, joy and hope in my heart could no longer be held back. The dam finally broke. I was at an age when people give up on life, and others around them also believe it is the last chapter of life. I took a leap of faith and decided to model POSSIBILITY:

- The possibility of always being young in thought & attitude;

- The possibility of breaking all myths related to age,

- The possibility of senior citizens using technology and social channels to connect instead of being technophobic

- The possibility of living it up and celebrating life and love every moment

- The possibility of creating a global community based on love, respect, sharing and connection

And Poonam Kalra 60, my YouTube Channel was born.

I am overwhelmed by all the love and respect I receive.

Friends, through my social channels and this book, I am sharing with you a blueprint of 360-degree prosperity encompassing Physical, Emotional, Mental and Spiritual Health, Relationship Harmony, Personal Development, Complete Confidence and Grooming.

I have shared with you all my personal recommendations and have only shared tools and techniques or traditional wisdom that I have tried and tested and those that have given me incredible results.

So, friends, here are the priceless secrets to your best life. Let's all share in the love, wisdom and joy and **"LIVE it Up!"**

Chapter 2

Change The Way You Eat To Change The Way You Feel!

Friends, we all know that Good Health is the root of our happiness and overall Well Being. We are taught this right from the beginning of our lives, that Health is our biggest Gift and our true wealth. Yet, most of us tend to take our Health for granted.

That is why whenever I connect with you all; I always make it a point to remind you of the importance of taking care of your Health.

All that I have achieved in life has been possible only due to good Health!

Health is a state of complete physical, mental, social and spiritual Wellbeing, which consists of regular maintenance of the body by following daily practices and preventive measures to avoid the possibility of diseases.

Health plays a significant role in keeping us prosperous and financially wealthy because we cannot be productive without Health.

Without Health; Life is a ZERO

Success in every area of your life is dependent on good Health. If you are not healthy, you cannot:

- Good care of your family.

- Be productive at work.

- Enjoy activities with your children.

- Socialize or have fun with friends and family.

- Contribute to society in any form.

Without good Health, NOTHING
is POSSIBLE! LIFE becomes ZERO

To lead a healthy life, you need a combination of a healthy and balanced diet, some form of exercise, weight management, and stress management activities.

Friends, I take my Health very seriously and work on it religiously. Here I am delighted to share my tried and tested health tips with you.

I only share what I have tried practically and what has benefitted me enormously. I share nothing theoretical. All that I share is tried, tested and proven.

In this section, in this and the following chapters, I will share with you in detail about healthy habits, weight management without side effects, stress management, diet plans, and healthy recipes.

Try these 7 things, and your life will never be the same!

1. **Say no to Refined Oils X:** Refined Oils are those that are refined or have been altered by using chemicals that are harmful to us.

The refinement process means that the oil might be treated with acid or purified with an alkali. It could have been neutralized, filtered or even deodorized. All these processes require harmful chemicals.

While being extracted from their seeds, oils sometimes get oxidized and may change into unhealthy Trans Fats. To remove the resulting smell, the oil is bleached to deodorize it.

Instead, use Natural Oils like Mustard or Olive.

I personally vouch for **MUSTARD OIL!**

Friends, I have personally shifted to Mustard Oil and seen the difference in my Health.

There are many benefits of using Mustard Oil as a cooking medium.

- ✓ It contains omega-3 and omega-6 fatty acids and has a low content of saturated fats.

- ✓ It is also useful in curing many skin, joints, muscles and even heart ailments.

- ✓ It contains rich amounts of monounsaturated and polyunsaturated fatty acids (MUFA and PUFA). These fats lower the risk of developing heart disease by almost half.

- ✓ Mustard oil is also said to have cancer-fighting properties.

2. **Say no to Added Salt X:** While Salt is truly the spice of life, having it in moderation is the key to a great life.

Salt in a certain amount is necessary for taste and health reasons. However, an excess can ruin taste as well as Health.

Excess Salt (both cooked & uncooked) can lead to:

- High Blood Pressure
- Osteoporosis
- Asthma
- Stomach Cancer
- Weight Gain
- Excess uncooked Salt has been linked to:
- Heart Disease
- Kidney Problems

Once Salt is cooked, it changes its Iron structure and becomes easy to absorb.

So, friends, I request you keep your salt in moderation and especially say no to added uncooked Salt always!

Also, friends, our table salt is fortified with Iodine. A certain amount of Iodine is needed for our body, but excess can be bad, so use table Salt in combination with a healthier variety, Rock Salt.

Here is my personal tried & tested formula for using Salt; Use Salts in combination:

Use 60% Iodized Table Salt +40% Rock Salt=Balanced Health

3. **Cut Down on Carbs:** Carbs, though necessary for energy, can be bad in excess and are difficult to digest. Especially cut down on refined carbs like Maida (refined Flour) & excessively refined Sugar, our body takes longer to digest these.

A simple formula is to:

Replace Everything *WHITE* with *BROWN*

Use Brown Bread, Brown Flour, and Brown Rice instead of white ones.

Avoid Sodas, Colas, Pastries and Pastas in excess.

Refined Carbs are stripped of all nutrients and can put you at risk of many diseases.

4. **Add Citrus Fruits and Berries to your Diet:** Friends, it is a must for you to add Citrus Fruits like Limes, Lemons, Oranges, Grapefruits etc. & Berries like Gooseberry, Blackberry etc. to your daily diet because:

    ✓ They are rich in Vitamins, especially C

    ✓ They are rich in Antioxidants

    ✓ They are low in calories

    ✓ They are a good source of fiber

    ✓ They reduce the risk of Kidney Stones

    ✓ They are Anti-Cancerous

    ✓ They boost Heart Health

    ✓ They help prevent diseases like Alzheimer's & Parkinson's

5. **Wake up to Water:** If I had to give you just one tip, friends, it would be this: wake up to Water and have it throughout the day.

    Drink Water first thing in the morning, 2 glasses if you can. Drinking water first thing in the morning flushes out your stomach. This improves our immune system.

- ✓ Drink at least 7–8 glasses of Water throughout the day. It helps
- ✓ Flush out Toxins
- ✓ Enhances Oxygenation
- ✓ Aids Digestion
- ✓ Normalizes Blood Pressure
- ✓ Stabilizes Heartbeat
- ✓ Regulates Body Temperature
- ✓ Keeps Joints in Working Order

6. **Eat a Banana Early in the Morning:** A Banana in the Morning is as Good as Gold!

   It's rich in nutrients, minerals, fiber & antioxidants, and it helps regulate Blood Pressure & Blood Sugar Levels.

   A Banana also improves digestive & heart Health and promotes a feeling of satiation that prevents overeating.

7. **Have Dinner Latest by 8.00 P.M.:** Having your dinner at least 2.5–3 hours before bedtime is necessary to give you time to digest it. Otherwise, it can play havoc with your system.

   - ✓ An early dinner is helpful in:
   - ✓ Aiding Digestion
   - ✓ Relieving Constipation
   - ✓ Relief from Gastritis
   - ✓ Weight Management
   - ✓ Improves Sleep

Friends, if you follow these tips regularly and build them into your life, I guarantee you that your life will change. Your digestion will be better, your oxygen levels will improve, and you will feel more energized, and you will be glowing with good Health.

You will be able to carry out all your activities joyfully and productively!

Chapter 3

Watch That Weight Friends!

Friends Weight Management is a huge part of being healthy! Being overweight can lead to a number of complications that you would never imagine, such as:

- High Blood Pressure (Hypertension)
- Risk of Heart Disease & Stroke
- Diabetes
- Gall Bladder & Kidney Concerns
- High Bad Cholesterol Levels
- Body pain, Joint pain/Swelling and Difficulty with Movement and Functioning
- Sleep Issues
- Breathing problems
- Depression, Anxiety, Panic etc.

Being overweight can lead to a low quality of physical, mental and emotional life. You are unable to participate fully in even the simple activities of life with your loved ones because of your pain & lessened mobility. This leads to an emotional conflict in relationships and then to mental health concerns.

Friends, I understand your concerns, and here I am sharing my simple and easy to use positive ways that will keep you at a healthy weight without starving yourself or tiring yourself out at the gym.

The first thing that I want to remind you of again is the 7 tips shared in chapter 1.

If you follow those 7 tips and incorporate them into your life daily, they will not only keep your general Health and vitality at a high level. They will also help in keeping your weight at an optimum level.

Other than these tips, friends I will share more simple yet effective methods that I have formulated personally and experienced their amazing results myself.

Water; The Master of Wellness

Having plain Water early in the morning and throughout the day alone is good enough, but friends, if you turn that Water into *Infused Detox Waters,* the magic of wellness gets doubled!

The real secret is to keep rotating your detox waters because if you keep drinking just one kind of detox water, then your body gets used to it, and you become immune to its benefits.

Also, another special secret tip for you; a great way to double your benefits is to have 2 kinds of detox water in a day, one early in the morning and one before lunch.

And here comes the real treasure for you; I am sharing with you, not just one, two or three kinds of Detox waters but 7 kinds of Detox waters for you to pick & choose from.

[The Recipes for these Detox Waters are given in detail in the Come Cook with Me, Recipe section on Page Number # 18]

Battle that Belly Fat and Win

While watching our weight, the most stubborn enemy is Belly Fat. It is easier to drop weight from the rest of the body but dropping Belly Fat is a real challenge.

Friends, if you add and modify these 10 things to your diet, you are sure to win the Battle of Belly Fat!

1. Add Oats &/or *Daliya* (Broken Wheat Porridge) to your diet on a daily basis. Either with milk (avoid Sugar, add a little honey if you have to) or cooked in minimum oil with Salt and vegetables.

2. Add a variety of Seeds like Chia, Flax, Sesame, Sunflower, and Pumpkin etc., to your daily diet.

3. If you are a Non-vegetarian, avoid meats, enhance Fish & Eggs in your diet. Stick to Egg Whites mostly; you can have the Egg Yellow once in a while, though.

4. Add/increase a lot of Green Veggies, especially fresh seasonal ones, in your diet.

5. Add Quinoa to your diet. Ensure you have it once in two days at least.

6. Add *Saunf* (Annie Seed), *Daalchini* (Cinnamon) and *Ajwain* (Thymol/Carom Seed) to your diet.

7. Make sure that you have Tomatoes and Cucumbers as Salad every day. They are low in calories and high in minerals and antioxidants.

8. Add Apples and Papaya to your diet. The new Mantra is this: ***An Apple with some Papaya a day keeps the Fat & the Doctor away!***

9. Go Nuts; I mean, add nuts to your diet. Almonds and Walnuts are the best, but you can add some Cashew in moderation too.

10. Make your Breakfast Protein Rich, Your Lunch Fiber Rich and keep your Dinner as Light and as Early as possible.

Create your Personal Portable Sauna at Home

As I already said earlier, friends, all my tips will be simple and easy to use, so here is one that you can do right at home while continuing with your daily routine and get all the fat-burning benefits of a world-class sauna.

Use this super simple secret trick in the following simple steps:

- After using the washroom in the morning, rub a little Vicks Vaoporub (it's generally always a staple in all Indian households) gently around your navel.

- Then a clean, pure cotton cloth at least 10 inch width and enough in length to be wrapped around your stomach twice at least.

- After applying the Vicks, wrap this cotton cloth tightly (allowing yourself breathing space) around your stomach. Make sure to cover your navel and abdomen area like a broad belt.

- Put on your regular clothes over this and carry on with your regular daily routine.

- Soon you will start sweating, and it will cause the extra fat to burn away from your body.

- Wear this for half an hour at least. Keep it for longer if you can.

However, friends, please note that this is not a miracle; this process takes time to work. After all, this excess fat wasn't accumulated in a few days, so how can you expect it to disappear in a few days?

Stick with this process for a month. Don't fret and measure or weigh yourself on a daily basis. Do so after a month, and you will see a marked difference.

The Healthy Quick Weight Management Diet Plan

Friends, this is my go-to magic diet plan whenever my weight gets out of control.

The best part is that this plan is completely healthy, has no side effects, and you will always be satiated. You won't be left feeling hungry and starved. So let's dive into the plan right away.

On waking up (Latest by 7.00 A.M.)	Have two glasses of Water without brushing your teeth. *You can have any of the Detox Waters suggested in the Recipe Section of the Book on Page 18. *If you find it difficult to have 2 glasses of Water first thing in the morning, start small. Begin with ½–1 glass and slowly go to 2 glasses.
After ½ an hour, Morning Tea	Have Tea along with 3 Almonds & 1 Walnut soaked overnight. *The Tea can be your regular *Desi Chai*, Black Tea or Green Tea. *Avoid Sugar

Breakfast (Latest by 9.30)	*Absolutely No *Parathas* or anything fried. Have either *Oats/Daliya/Uppma/Poha/Idli/Chilla (either Besan, Moong Dal, Oats, Suji)*/Brown Bread Sandwich/Eggs. *In case you crave Jam, you can have one slice of Brown Bread with Jam.
12.00 Noon	One serving of either Apple or Papaya or both. *Do not have anything other than these 2 fruits.
Around 1.30–2.00 P.M. (half an hour before Lunch)	A salad consisting majorly of Tomatoes & Cucumber
Lunch (Latest by 2.30 P.M.)	1 Big Bowl *Lauki Sabzi* (Cooked Bottle Gourd) + 1 *Chapati* + 1 Glass of *Chaach* (Buttermilk) *The Buttermilk should be had at the end of the meal.
Evening Snack 5.30 P.M.	Have Tea along with *Murmure* (Puffed Rice)/ Roasted *Makhane* (Fox Nuts)/Single Slice Brown Bread Sandwich/1 Boiled Egg *The Tea can be your regular *Desi Chai*, Black Tea or Green Tea. *Avoid Sugar
Dinner (Latest by 8.00 P.M.)	1–1.5 Bowl of Vegetable Soup + 1 Slice of Brown Bread. *No Butter on your Bread or in your Soup.
Bed Time 10.00 P.M.	1 Cup Turmeric Milk with no sugar.

*In case you have to wake up till 11.00–12.00 P.M. and fall prey to hunger pangs, again eat only a small serving of Papaya.

Exercise

The Critical Ingredient in Weight Management

Now friends here is the most special tip not just for weight management but also for overall physical & mental Wellbeing.

No matter how much you alter your diet, nothing will give you complete results until you add some sort of physical exercise to the mix.

Physical exercise is necessary to facilitate mobility, enhance digestion, increase oxygenation, build strength & stamina and decrease susceptibility to disease.

Exercising also releases endorphins, the feel-good hormone that fosters Wellbeing.

So friends, please ensure at least 30 minutes of physical exercise in your routine at least 4 times a week.

There are plenty of forms of exercise to choose from, you can do aerobics or Yoga if you like dancing you can dance your way to good Health and a slimmer fitter you. You can cycle if you know how to, it's a great way to exercise.

However, the best exercise is this: Walk your way to Wellbeing!

Walking is one of the simplest and best ways of exercising as it involves your whole body, needs no equipment, props or even music (of course, music makes walking even better, but it's not essential like it's to dancing).

Walking is something you can do when away on a trip too.

Also, you can walk even when you are confined to your home.

This is something I can personally vouch for. During the lockdown at the peak of the pandemic, my blood sugar levels were tested to be in the Prediabetic range, and I was deeply disheartened. However, my brother encouraged me and told me that I still had a chance to reverse this, else if it went up, I would be stuck with Diabetes medication for life.

He said he had full faith in me, so I researched and found that I could reverse this if I walked. Now it wasn't possible to go out during the lockdown. So I started walking in my garden.

5 minutes of walk equaled 500 steps, I kept walking for a few minutes after every few hours, and I managed to complete 6000 steps in a day. Thus continuing to walk at home, I brought down my sugar levels to the nondiabetic range.

Friends, you can walk at home anywhere, in your garden, lawn, veranda, driveway, terrace, balcony, and even in the largest room in your house if there is no other usable space in your home.

If you can't walk at one go, you can break it up. Walk for 15 or so minutes every few hours.

If I had to tell you only one thing to do in life, friends, it would definitely be walking.

Chapter 4

Cook With Me;
Eat Healthy, Stay Healthy!

Friends, as promised in this section, I invite you into my kitchen to share some easy, healthy recipes that will help you on your mission to being fit and energetic and enjoying life thoroughly.

Let's cook together and have fun being fit!

Let's start this section with the treasure house of:

7 Detox Waters!

Saunf (Annie/Fennel Seed) Water

Soak 2 TBSPs of *Saunf* in 1.5 glasses of Water. Boil and reduce it to 1 glass in the morning and drink it warm or cool it and drink.

Lemon Peel Water

Add peels of 1–2 Lemons (after you have used the juice) in 1.5 glasses of Water. Boil and reduce it to 1 glass in the morning and drink it warm or cool it and drink.

Ajwain (Thymol/Carom Seed) Water

Soak 1.5 TBSPs of *Ajwain* in 1.5 glasses of Water. Boil and reduce it to 1 glass in the morning and drink it warm or cool it and drink.

Lemon Water with a Twist

Keep a Lemon in the freezer for a while, then grate it whole and add it to a glass of Water at room temperature and drink it.

Ginger Water

Grate a 1 piece of Ginger, add it to 1.5 glasses of Water. Boil and reduce it to 1 glass and drink it warm or cool it and drink. Add a little honey to this as the Ginger tastes rather sharp.

Methi Dana (Fenugreek Seed) Water

Soak 1.5 TBSPs of *Methi Dana* in 1.5 glasses of Water. Boil and reduce it to 1 glass in the morning and drink it warm or cool it and drink.

Curry Leaf Water

Add 8–10 Curry Leaves in 1.5 glasses of Water. Boil and reduce it to 1 glass and drink it warm or cool it and drink.

Raitas to the Rescue
Two Delicious Healthy Curd Based Accompaniments

Curd is an important part of our diet. It is a natural Probiotic. It can be taken in various forms. Here I am sharing with you two variations, both Sweet and Savory, but both extremely healthy.

1 Cup of Curd, add 3 TBSPs of Chia Seeds and 1 TBSP of Oats to it and keep it in the fridge overnight.

The next day divide it into two parts; dilute it with a bit of water and whisk it to a smooth consistency.

The Savory *Raita*

To one part, add diced onions, cucumber, tomatoes, mint and green coriander to it, add Salt and pepper to taste, and your yummy *Raita* is ready.

Use it either as an accompaniment to Lunch or as a healthy snack anytime.

The Sweet *Raita*

Whisk the other part with a little water and a few pinches of sugar to a smooth consistency. Add a few pieces of diced apple, mango, banana, pineapple or a few grapes. Top it with a little **Anaar Dana** (Pomegranate Seeds), and your yummy **Raita** is ready.

Use it either as an accompaniment to Lunch, as a healthy snack or even as a dessert.

Success with Soups

Soups are a great way to keep you nourished and healthy while keeping light and fit. So friends, please try out these easy yet amazingly satisfying soups to stay healthy.

Home Style Mixed Vegetable Soup

Ingredients

- 4 Piece of *Lauki* (Bottle Gourd)
- ½ a medium-sized Carrot
- 2 medium-sized Tomatoes
- 3–4 cloves of Garlic

Method

i. Chop all the ingredients roughly. Pressure cook them for about 7 minutes with 1.5 glasses of Water. Strain, keep the stock (Water) aside. Blend the cooked vegetables and strain them again. Put the blended veggies into the stock, add Salt to taste and bring to a boil. Finish it with a dash of freshly ground pepper and your Soul food is ready.

Home Style Mixed Lentil Soup

Ingredients

- 2 TBSP *Moong Dhuli Dal*
- 2 TBSP *Masoor Dhuli Dal*
- 2 TBSP *Arhar/Toor Dal*
- 2 TBSP *Chana Dal*
- 1 medium-sized Tomato
- 3–4 cloves of Garlic

Method

i. Chop the Tomato and add all the ingredients together with 1.5 glasses of Water. Pressure cook them for about 7 minutes. Strain, keep the stock (Water) aside. Blend the cooked ingredients all together. Add Salt to taste and bring to a boil. Finish it with a dash of freshly ground pepper, and your Soul food is ready.

Smoothen your Health with an Awesome Smoothie!

Friends, Smoothies are a great way to put together healthy ingredients and make them into a healthy, tasty and attractive meal in a glass.

Here is a simple smoothie recipe that you can add to your breakfast or have as a snack anytime.

Ingredients

- 1 Glass of Low Fat Milk
- 1 Banana
- 2 Almonds, soaked overnight and peeled
- 2–3 TBSPs of Chia Seeds
- A pinch of Black Pepper and a pinch of Cinnamon

Method

i. Blend all the ingredients together to a smooth consistency, and your healthy smoothie is ready.

ii. *You can replace the Banana with a fruit of your choice.

iii. Homemade French Fries

Ingredients

- 2 medium-sized Potatoes
- Oil for frying
- Salt to taste

Method

i. Chop the potatoes into long finger-like pieces.

ii. Soak them in chilled Water for 10 minutes. Strain them after 10 minutes and transfer them to hot, salted Water for 10 minutes.

iii. Strain them and pat dry on a kitchen towel. Transfer to a freezer-safe dish and freeze for an hour.

iv. Take them out, heat the oil in a wok/pan and fry them till crisp.

v. Add Salt, pepper, or any other **Masala** that you would like, and your restaurant style fries are ready without the side effects and health dangers.

Chapter 5

Bonus Health Tips To Make Life Better!

Friends at one time or the other, we have all been given simple health tips by Doctors, little things that make a big difference to our health and, consequently, our quality of life.

However, we often tend to miss what is simple and easy. That's why I want to remind you of these simple things. Together let's pledge to build all these changes into our lives gradually.

Drink at least 8–10 glasses of water a day. Our grandmothers have been telling us all along, and all fields of medicine, ayurvedic & allopathic, recommend this, but most of us forget to do this.

If having just plain cold water is challenging, then add some fun to it. Cut some fruits or veggies & herbs such as cucumber, coriander, mint etc. leave them in your drinking water for some time and drink this flavoured infused water.

Nimbu paani (lemonade), green tea, fruit juices (fresh, not processed packaged ones), and buttermilk are also great options to increase your liquid intake.

Your medicines only with plain water at room temperature. Taking them with anything else or at hot or cold temperatures can cause them to change chemically and be less effective or even have side effects sometimes.

Sleep on your left side as much as possible, as it puts less pressure on your organs and aids digestion.

Have at least one helping of seasonal fruits every day. Make sure to include citrus fruits and berries in it as well. This will give you a healthy dose of vitamins and minerals and help build immunity.

Build some stress busters like Yoga, Meditation or Gardening into your daily routine. While Yoga & Meditation have been proven to calm the mind and body since ancient times. Gardening is also a great stress buster as it brings you in contact with nature. Watching your plants grow and communicating with them fills you up with positivity.

Always have your meals hot or warm (or at room temperature at least). Never have them cold out of the fridge. Not even salads should be had cold. Also, salads and fruits should never be cut & kept. They should be cut fresh and eaten instantly.,

Walk at least 20 minutes a day. The benefits of walking can never be overemphasized. It improves circulation, oxygenation and mobility.

Say no to French Fries made commercially. French Fries are the most popular food worldwide; they are tasty and comforting, also easy to eat on the go.

However, Doctors and Health experts advise people to avoid commercially made French Fries as these are fried in the same oil repeatedly at extremely high temperatures, which causes the oil to turn to poison literally.

I am not saying you should not eat or give French Fries to your children. Just don't give them the ones that are made commercially in restaurants and diners.

Make French Fries at home; they are easy and simple to make. I have shared my Home Style French Fry Recipe with you in the Cook with Me section on Page # 18.

This recipe will give you restaurant-style fries minus all the dangerous side effects.

Friends with this, we come to the end of the section on health. I sincerely wish that together we will all follow these easy to use dietary, exercise and lifestyle changes and multiply our happiness.

MIND OVER MATTER!
CLAIM YOUR MENTAL
& EMOTIONAL WEALTH!

Chapter 6

Invest In Yourself!

Keep Your Cup Full

Friends, if I asked you to list your favourite people, very few of you would put your name at the top of that list.

How sad is that!

Every single thing, every relationship in this universe exists because we do! If we cannot love ourselves, how can we love others? It is a well-known fact that we can pour a cup of Tea only from a full kettle.

So in our lives, we can only spread love and happiness to others only when we are happy and full of love.

Therefore friends, remember to keep your cup full so you can share it with others. Work on improving yourself and making yourself the best version of yourself because you are your true wealth. Invest in yourself.

Let me share with you 8 wonderful ways to improve yourself and enhance your emotional and mental Wellbeing.

8 Habits for an Improved New You!

1. **Ensure that you perform an act of kindness or goodness every day,** offer to help someone, guide someone, or be of service to someone in some way. An act of selfless service will make you feel good about yourself.

2. **Wake up early. It gives you more time to be productive,** and it infuses you with more energy. If you are not used to waking up early, you won't be able to do it suddenly. So do it gradually, start by moving up the time by ½ an hour slowly until you manage to get up at your desired time.

3. **Make sure you give your 100% to whatever you do.** When you do something with dedication, it gives you better results and leaves you feeling satisfied and happy.

4. **Learn something from your friends.** We all have different kinds of friends; each of these friends has unique positive qualities. Meet your friends frequently and choose at least one quality from each of them and try to imbibe and cultivate that quality within you. This way, you will be able to develop a number of new skills and qualities.

5. **Just as it's necessary to develop positive qualities,** it is extremely important to protect your energy and avoid negative and toxic people. They can demotivate you and drain you off all your energy.

6. **Standing with your friends, family,** and extended family during their challenging times and celebrating with them in their good times shape your personality too. It makes you a better person.

7. **Do not spread yourself thin by trying to please everyone.** It is a well-known fact that can never please everyone all the time. Trying to do this will only stress you out. So just make sure that you do your best in everything you do. If that pleases people great, if not, be happy that you did your best.

8. **You must work on developing patience.** Patience is one of the best qualities one can have. Patience keeps us motivated toward our goals instead of wanting instant results. Patience helps keep relationships together and allows us to stay calm in irritating or disturbing situations.

Friends, if you work on building these 8 habits into your life. You will always be calm, relaxed, and happy instead of irritable, dissatisfied, sad, and angry.

Chapter 7

Affirm The Life
That You Want!

Affirmations are Divine Universal Truths!

Friends here, I share with you an extremely simple yet powerful spiritual practice that can miraculously transform your life if you practice it patiently and correctly.

Affirmations are short phrases beginning with *"I AM"* that affirm a positive thought, desire, goal, emotion, or experience. These phrases are always in the present tense because the present is all that matters.

Work on the Subconscious Mind

These phrases, when spoken with feelings and emotions, set into motion universal vibrations. These affirmations work at two levels. First, at the conscious level, by repeatedly telling your subconscious mind the same thing over and over, you are making your mind believe that truth.

Say, for example, if you are not rich, but you want to become rich. Then when you start by affirming that **"I AM RICH,"** your conscious mind will initially not believe you. However, when you keep repeating it for a significant period, you will begin to accept it as the truth. The next step will communicate this to the subconscious mind, and the subconscious mind will also believe this. Now the subconscious mind will start working to make it a reality and guide you toward ideas, opportunities, and actions aligned with your goal to give you the desired results.

Once your subconscious mind believes what you are affirming, that belief begins to seep into your subconscious mind, and then your subconscious mind starts guiding your mind and actions to align with your desired goal.

Now, friends, you may be having so many questions about affirmations. Let me answer them for you one by one.

What can I Affirm about?

Affirmations can be used in every area of your life, be it your job, business, relationships, finances, health, or any other area of your life.

What is the best time to Affirm?

As soon as you wake up in the morning is a great time to affirm because it sets the tone for the day. Also, first thing in the morning, your energy is unpolluted, and your connection to the universal energy is strong.

Just before going to bed when our mind is drifting between the conscious and the subconscious is a great time to affirm as it allows the affirmations to be absorbed deep into your subconscious mind.

Other than this, anytime during the day is an excellent time to use your affirmations. However, whenever you use your affirmations, make sure that you are entirely focused on them.

How Many Affirmations Can I Use?

Friends, there is divided opinion on how many affirmations can be used at a time. Some people believe there is no capping on the number of affirmations that can be used at a time. While others believe only limited affirmations should be used at a time.

Since I only share with you what has shown me results let me share how I use affirmations.

I suggest you focus on one or two areas of your life and work on them until you get the desired results and then address the next area priority-wise.

Also, friends, I suggest that it is best to use 4–7 affirmations at any one time.

For How Long Should I Use Affirmations?

It is often suggested that affirmations should be used for at least 21 days. Popular thought also puts the number at 28 and 45 days, respectively.

But friends, again, I have a tried and tested suggestion to make. Don't be focused on the number of days; just affirm with belief, conviction, and feeling. Visualize it as you affirm and let the magic unfold organically. Have patience. If you do right, the results will follow.

You can keep doing it lifelong, too, to maintain and sustain the results you have achieved.

What do I say while Affirming?

You are completely free to affirm anything you want. Use your words the way you want. However, to get you started, I am sharing some examples of powerful affirmations for the important areas of your life here:

Money

- Money comes to me easily and effortlessly.
- I am a money magnet.
- I attract opportunities that create more money.
- I am worthy and deserving of making money.
- I am open and receptive to all avenues of making money.
- My actions are always aligned toward prosperity.
- Money and spirituality can co-exist in harmony.

Love & Relationships

- I am full of positive, loving energy.
- I am loved, loving and lovable.
- I welcome love and romance into my life.
- I am in a loving and supportive relationship.
- I deserve love.
- I am blessed with an incredible family and wonderful friends.
- I am surrounded by loving and supportive people.

Health

- I deserve to be healthy and feel good.
- I am filled with energy and vitality to the brim.
- I am getting healthier and stronger every day.
- I honor my body and listen to it.
- I always make healthy choices.

Happiness

- I am grateful to be alive.

- Happiness is my birthright. I choose to be happy, and I deserve to be happy.

- Being happy comes easy to me. Happiness is my second nature.

- I am deeply fulfilled by what I do.

Personal

- My possibilities are endless.

- I am good enough.

- I am worthy of my dreams.

- I am becoming the best version of myself.

- I have the freedom, resources & power to create the life I desire.

- I choose to be kind to myself and love myself unconditionally.

Keep in Mind while Affirming

1. Just repeating them mechanically will not make them useful, and you will not achieve any results.

2. Also, when using affirmations, ensure that your spirits are high and you are operating out of positive energy. If you say affirm from a place of disbelief or desperation, they will never work, friends.

3. You must always affirm in the present tense, never in the future. If you affirm in the future, the result will always stay in the future. Let me show you an example. When you say **"I AM RICH,"** you are declaring to the universe and your mind that you are rich right now, right here, not somewhere down the future. But if you affirm

that "**I WILL BE RICH**," you are telling them that you will be rich in the future. So it always stays in the future.

4. If you use affirmations with the intent to harm anyone, they will never give you results.

So friends, go ahead and transform your life with the power of affirmations!

Chapter 8

Unlock The Miracles of The Subconscious Mind!

The Real Mastermind

Friends, we can only be truly happy and in control of our life when we learn to tap into and harness the power of the subconscious mind.

Our conscious mind works only when we actively think, act, or consider a decision, and it works only 10%. In contrast, our subconscious mind is the real Mastermind, which does 90% of the work and never rests; it works 24×7 all 365 days.

When we sleep, the conscious mind stops working, but the subconscious mind doesn't rest even then.

The conscious mind is more oriented toward facts, analysis, thinking and logic, while the subconscious mind operates based on emotions, experiences, feelings and memories.

Feeding The Subconscious Mind

We, as human beings, tend to think the worst of everything. We always imagine the worst possible scenarios. We jump to negative conclusions before we look at the positive aspects.

Friends, I have already shared with you how the subconscious mind takes information from the conscious mind, stores it and then works toward making it a reality.

So when we keep thinking negatively, that is what we are feeding our subconscious mind and it turns that into reality.

When we think negatively, the subconscious mind works overtime to feed our conscious mind with negativity and align it toward negative actions and experiences. Then we remain upset the whole day.

Turn It Around

But friends, what if you used the power of the subconscious mind to your advantage.

What if we feed it more positivity? Then it would align our thoughts, ideas, actions and experiences toward happiness and positivity only.

What we feed our subconscious mind in the few minutes before we go to sleep is of utmost importance. Usually, we do that before going to sleep. We think of all the things that went wrong throughout the day, which the subconscious mind stores and works upon.

The next day it gives us more things that go wrong! So before going to bed, use this very special technique that I do and watch how your life changes.

A Healthy Diet For Your Subconscious Mind

Friends, when I lie down on my bed, I breathe in through my nose and out through my mouth deeply, and I visualize that I am breathing in positivity and clarity and breathing out negativity and confusion.

Then I plug in my earphones, and *I listen to the affirmations of positivity, desires and goals that I have recorded in my voice and then to a special plan I have made for the next day* of what I will do and how I will act. And listening to these, I drift off to sleep.

This gives my subconscious mind the whole night to prepare my mind for a positive, happy and productive experience the next day.

If you cannot record for some reason (although I recommend you make an effort for yourself), then make sure that you think these positive thoughts and plans before going to sleep.

You might have heard many times that people say I woke up very happy and energized today, or some other people say that I had this brilliant idea when I woke up in the morning today.

All this happens when they go to sleep with positive thoughts instead of focusing on negative ones.

So, friends, it's time to tap into the power of the subconscious mind, control of your life, and shape it the way you want.

Chapter 9

Mindfulness,
Let's Live In The Present!

Open your Present

To live a happy and contented life, we must let go of the past and live in the present.

Friends, the present is truly a *"Present"* from the almighty. It is a precious gift for it teaches us to enjoy, value and focus on the present moment, eliminating unnecessary stress.

Whether it was good, bad or neutral, the past is the past and dwelling on it cannot change it. If the past was not good and we are in a better place now, then we will be unable to enjoy even the happiness we have now. If we have happy memories of the past, we must cherish them but not spend all our time on them and neglect our present.

If we have made any mistakes in the past, we should learn from them and move on instead of staying in the past and wallowing in guilt.

Similarly, worrying about the future will stress you out too. Planning for the future is good but worrying about it is not, because it will do nothing except spoil your present.

We should always be mindful of being in the present and enjoying it, focusing on it and being grateful for it.

Accept what you can't Change

Friends, there are certain things in life that we can't change and certain things that we can change. Most often, instead of changing the things that we can, we keep focusing on and struggling against the things we can change.

This causes us unnecessary stress and worry. What we can change is our behaviour, responses and actions to things, but we don't focus on that.

Once we change our response, the results immediately change.

We must accept the things that we can't change like we accept the weather. If it is summer, we don't fight it and ask it not to be hot; Instead; we change our response; we dress lighter, use fans, ACs and drink more water.

If it is Winter, we accept it and wear woollen clothes, drink warm beverages.

If we could do this with people and situations, we could be so much happier. Like our relatives, we can't change them, and we can't avoid them altogether. Some are nice, some we gel with, some are mean, and some are annoying. However, once we accept them for who they are and stop resisting them, we will be so much happier.

However, with friends, we sometimes do the opposite. Friends are people we choose, and sometimes we make an error of judgement, and some of them may not be genuine friends, but we keep sticking to them in the name of loyalty. Friends, here we have a choice. We can and should do away with the toxic people around us.

So if we are mindful of accepting what we can't change and changing what we can, then we can definitely live a calm, stress-free life.

Be Mindful of the Bitter Truths of Life

While there are so many wonderful things about life, we cannot ignore the duality of life. The good and bad, night and day, creation and destruction, black and white... these are all realities of life

To be truly happy, we must accept and be mindful of some bitter truths of life.

- When you are going through a low phase in life, especially in terms of money, 90% of your friends and relatives will desert you.

- That no one lives a fairy tale life all the time, at some point of their life (and sometimes multiple times), everyone goes through a period of struggle.

- Nobody is perfect, so accept yourself and others with all their shades of grey.

- Trust is precious, don't trust anyone blindly. Always be alert, for often, it is those closest to you that betray you.

So promise me, friends, that you will live life mindfully in a calm, relaxed and stress-free environment from today onward.

Chapter 10

Dealing With Negativity, Anger & Addiction

Friends, it is necessary to keep our mind free of negativity and to keep it strong. For that, we have to keep some things at bay, such as Negative thoughts and feelings, Anger and addictive behaviour.

No To Negativity

We all have something in common; none of us is perfect. Even people who are full of great qualities will still have a few shortcomings. But as we have discussed earlier, we as human beings tend to focus only on the negative. In comparison, we must train our mind to focus only on the positive.

In the earlier chapters of this section, I have shared with you some wonderful tools such as affirmations, meditations for the subconscious mind, yoga etc.

Here I am sharing with you two special techniques that will help you stay positive throughout the day, and positivity will then become a habit one day at a time.

Don't Wake Up To Your Phone

Usually, these days, we wake up to our phone, and that's wonderful because it allows us to connect with friends and family and receive their wishes for the day.

However, before we connect with anyone else, it is more important to connect with ourselves, so friends don't wake up to your phone; wake up to yourself and your connection with your creator.

Journey Within To Gratitude

- As soon as you wake up, friends, try to sit peacefully in a quiet place and breathe deeply.

- Breathe in deeply through your nose and visualize positivity going in and breathe out through your mouth, visualizing the negativity flowing out.

- Then express thanks to the almighty and give gratitude for being lucky enough to see another day.

- Then express gratitude to your parents for having given birth to you and for having nurtured you.

- Express gratitude for your family and friends and for the home that you live in.

- Express your love and gratitude for your body for carrying out all the necessary functions smoothly.

- Express gratitude for your sound mind.

- Express gratitude for the food you are blessed with to sustain life.

- Express gratitude for all the sources of income you are blessed with.

- Sit quietly with your eyes closed for some time, allowing the miracle of gratitude & positivity to seep into your mind and body.

- Then affirm that I will only see, feel, do and receive good today. I will only allow positivity into my aura.

Hello Beautiful!

- After practicing your morning gratitude ritual, go into the bathroom or any other place with a mirror and stand in front of it. Look at your reflection in the mirror.

- Greet the person in the mirror with a smile.

- Talk to your reflection in the mirror. Tell them "I am proud of you."

- "I believe in you."

- Today is the best day of your life till now.

- Today is full of positivity and happiness.

- You will do our best work to date today.

- You are lucky to be seeing this day.

Now you are free to go ahead and check your phone and check into your daily world. Have a great day, friends!

Your Mind is Stronger Than Your Addiction

Addiction, the word in itself, feels so heavy. But friends, it is a reality of life. Many of us are addicted to some things in life; there are various sorts of addictions. Addiction to substances, smoking, alcohol, gadgets, social media, coffee, chocolate, even shopping.

Addictions make us their slaves. They weaken our minds and resolve. Friends, however, at some point or the other, we reach a stage where we are sick of being a slave to our addiction and of being so weak, and in that moment of weakness lies our strength.

In those few seconds, if you decide you have had enough and you decide to quit, believe me, friends, it will be permanent.

However, if you think I will quit tomorrow or set a time that I will stop from a particular day, it will never happen.

So when the trick to quitting is right when you are triggered by it.

Once you have decided to quit, depending on the type and severity of addiction, you must ensure you seek any professional help necessary. Also, you must ensure that you seek support from your family and friends and any other support groups.

If You Could See Yourself in Anger!

Friends, when we look at someone who is angry, how do we feel? We don't feel good. Why? Because their aura radiates negative vibes, their voice is harsh, their manner is rough and aggressive, and they look intimidating.

Friends, today I want to show you the same mirror. If we could all see how scary and terrible we all look when we are angry, we would choose to never be angry for even a second ever.

Also, tell me, friends, if we look at it wisely, there is never any need to get angry. If we are right, how is being angry going to be of any help, it will only make you seem unreasonable rather than right. If we are wrong, then of course, you have no business being angry.

Anger is not our natural state of being; we need to understand that in normal circumstances, anger has no impact on the situation. The message never reaches anyone. When we are angry, only 50% of people listen to us, not because they agree with us. Some of them agree because they are too weak to counter us. Others agree only to defuse the situation.

In contrast, when we speak lovingly, softly and reasonably, our message gets across almost 100% of the time.

However, friends, there are certain situations when we feel we are being hurt in an unjustifiable manner and for reasons of keeping the peace or out of respect for someone or due to cultural/traditional reasons we are unable to retort or retaliate. In such situations, though the ugliness is avoided you end up bottling the resentment, and that keeps you angry.

For that, I am sharing a very special and personal technique with you that will help you keep the peace and release the anger also.

Speak Out The Anger

- Friends in such a situation where you are hurt and angry but don't want to retaliate. Leave the situation.

- Go to a quiet, undisturbed place as soon as possible.

- Out your phone; switch on the video recording mode.

- Now vent out all that you would want to say in the situation, to the person, if you could.

- Don't hold anything back; let it all flow out till you feel completely done.

- Then watch that video and delete it.

- Drink a glass or two of water. It will calm you down.

- After a few minutes, have a cup/glass of your favourite beverage/drink, be it coffee, tea, milkshakes, lemonade etc. This will make you feel happy and positive.

- Now review your state of mind. You will be 95% back to normal with no anger or resentment.

- Now let me tell you the special ingredient that will make you 100% okay. Call and speak to a friend or relative who you are fond of and enjoy talking to.

- Have a normal conversation with them with no reference to the situation. You will feel on top of the world now!

Chapter 11

Bonus Tips To Calm
& Destress Your Mind

Friends, I share with you some bonus tips that will help you keep your mind calm & de-stressed and will keep you happy and positive always.

- Responsibility for your own happiness. Do not expect anyone else to make you happy.

- Never compare yourself to others. You are unique, and you are beautiful and amazing. There is no one like you. No one can do what you can. We are all special and beautiful in our own ways. A garden needs all sorts of flowers to be truly beautiful, so thus the world needs all kinds of people to make it beautiful.

- Don't let others' opinions and judgement about you drive your behaviour. Live life being true to yourself. Be YOU bravely, beautifully!

- Make time for your family and friends no matter how busy you are. It will keep you energized, de-stressed and happy always.

- Don't overthink. Look at the facts, process and analyze them but do not overthink situations and relationships.

Friends, I have shared with you all that has worked for me, and I sincerely hope you will use these to transform your life for lasting happiness and success.

SECTION 3

RELATIONSHIPS;
THE REASON FOR BEING!
LET'S BUILD OUR TREASURE!

Chapter 12

Becoming The Husband That Every Wife Wants

Friends, our primary relationship is with ourselves. Every other relationship exists because we do.

In the previous section of this book, I have already shared with you about loving and accepting yourself and keeping your cup of joy always full to serve others joy.

In this section of the book, I will share all that I have observed, learned and applied to my relationships to make them beautiful and smooth.

In this chapter, let's talk about the little things that a husband or partner can ensure to keep their spouses and partners happy so that the relationship is always alive, long-lasting, deep-rooted and enjoyable.

Traditionally a good husband is defined as one who earns well, provides for the family and takes care of the children's education. But friends, I agree with this definition of a good husband.

I have seen many husbands who fulfil these standard requirements, yet they insult their wives in public, in front of friends, family, staff etc., or provide them with all the material comforts but do not give them time and attention.

Honestly, friends, it really doesn't take much to make your wife/partner feel loved and cherished. If you take care of these little things, your relationship will be lasting and beautiful.

- **Respect your wife.** As your partner as well as an individual. Just as every human being deserves to be respected, so does your wife. When you choose to enter into a relationship, you invite the other partner on an equal platform. Do not ever insult her in public or even in front of the children or your parents. If there is something, you don't agree with or do not like. Tell her in private. She will love, respect and trust you more for it.

- **Accept her as she is.** When you marry someone or live with them, remember they already have a well-formed personality by then. Do not be over critical of her choices or behaviour. Over time you both will learn and understand each other's ways. Do not force her to do things your way.

- **Appreciate her;** please try and notice the little things about what she likes to eat and what makes her happy. Notice and appreciate any changes in her appearance, a new dress, a new haircut. Compliment her verbally too. Don't just notice and keep it to yourself. Compliment her on her cooking or any other skills that she has.

- **Value her opinion;** she is your most trusted well-wisher. Try and at least listen to her advice and opinions when she offers it. You may not see things from her point of view, but let her know that you welcome her opinion.

- **Involve her in decisions** that impact the family directly, such as buying a new house or a new car etc., even if you have researched it all… explain it to her and her input when you compare options. Don't just shrug off her inputs. This will make her feel valued and heard.

- **Encourage her to take independent decisions;** don't make her feel that she needs your permission for every little thing. She should not feel controlled. After all, she is your partner, not your property. Even if she asks you for permission for trivial things, tell her she doesn't need your permission for little things. Believe me, she will be so delighted, and her confidence will soar immediately.

- **Respect her parents** as it is not only she who is duty-bound to respect your parents. Parents, no matter who they are, always deserve respect. When you respect her parents, it makes her feel so proud of you and increases her love and respect for you manifold.

- **Let her work or run a business if she wants to.** Friends, I have seen many husbands and families discourage their wives from pursuing something they enjoy and are good at professionally. They often say we are so well off. Why should you work? We don't need the money. My dear friends, it's not about the money at all; it's about her self-expression and self-worth. It's about the fulfilment that comes from using her skills and exploring her potential.

- **Care for her when she is unwell.** If your wife falls ill or is a little unwell, you will, of course, take her to the doctor if needed, but friends; there are little things that you can do to make her show you care. Tell her she need not cook; you will rustle up something or call in. Offer to make her Tea and care for the kids so she can rest. Spend a little time sitting with her before going to work. She will appreciate your care deeply.

- **Hold hands with each other** while walking or when in the mall or park etc. Believe me; this little touch will strengthen your bond deeply. It allows your energies and auras to merge, which helps you understand and appreciate each other better.

Friends, if you make these little efforts for your relationship, believe me, your happiness will multiply manifold.

So go ahead and become the Husband every wife wants and wishes for and tell me how your wife thanks you for it.

Chapter 13

Being The Husband That Every Wife Wants

Friends, it is not the responsibility of just one partner to make the effort to keep the relationship alive and energized. A relationship can only work if both the people involved work at it.

So friends, in the previous chapter, I shared how husbands can keep their wives happy by taking care of little things. Now I will share how wives should ensure they keep the relationship happy and running smoothly.

- **Respect your Husband** as your partner as well as an individual. Do not ever argue with him in public or even in front of the children. If there is something, you don't agree with or do not like. Talk to him in private. He will love, respect and trust you more for it.

- **Keep a smiling face and dress well.** Your Husband already faces so many challenges and carries so many responsibilities on his shoulders. If he comes home to an ill-tempered and ill-kept wife, imagine how he would feel. When he comes home to a pleasant and smiling wife, he feels energized and ready to take on the world again.

- **The way to a man's heart is through his stomach.** This ancient nugget of wisdom has been passed down to us through generations by our grandmothers and friends. It is really true. Husbands love to be fed, so make sure to serve him warm, delicious meals of his liking, and he will be ever so grateful to you, and it will help deepen the relationship.

- **Compliment your Husband** whenever you notice something about his appearance or clothes or haircut or a thoughtful action or Gift toward you. It is not only a woman's privilege to be complimented. Men love being complimented too.

- **Respect his parents** as it shows that you respect him too. Parents, no matter who they are, always deserve respect. When you respect his parents, it makes him feel proud of you and increases his love and respect for you manifold.

- **Give your husband space.** It is very important. I often see that wives become very clingy and do not allow their husbands any me-time, or get very upset if they want to hang out with their friends or go on a trip with them. Ladies, please trust your Husband and set him free. Don't grudge him his time with his friends. Believe me, he will love and respect you even more for this, making your relationship better.

- **Don't talk ill of your Husband to anyone.** He is the person closest to you. He is someone you are likely to spend the major part of your life with. If you have any concerns talk to him directly and sort them out. Do not bitch about him to your friends or family.

- **Don't create a scene** if he is unable to stick to the plans you made together. If he has to cancel an outing or a dinner date due to sudden work commitments or feeling tired or unwell, many women throw a huge tantrum, adding to his tension. Believe me; he already feels guilty, don't make him feel worse. Assure him that it's okay and you can always go out another day.

- **Don't drag him into mom-in-law issues.** If you have any concerns with your mother-in-law, please try and sort them out between the two of you. You are both dear to him; don't make him choose between you.

Chapter 14

Becoming The Parents That Every Teenager Wishes For

The parent-child relationship is the most precious, yet it can also be the most difficult to navigate, especially when the children hit the teenage years.

Friends, here are some tried and tested tips that will make your relationship with your teenagers smooth. The key is to realize that they are their own individuals, and they deserve your respect too.

- **Don't ever share what they tell you with anyone.** Your children trust you and share with you things about themselves, their day and their friends. They should feel confident that what they tell you will stay with them. Otherwise, they will stop sharing with you.

- **Don't scold them for every little thing.** Choose your battles wisely. There will be some things where you will need to perhaps reprimand them for correcting them. However, scolding them for every little thing like breaking a glass or forgetting to do something or spilling food, etc., will only make them under confident and resent you.

- **Don't talk ill of your children to anyone.** This is the worst thing you can do. Even if they are wrong, you should correct them privately. Complaining to others is not going to solve anything. They will never trust you if you do this and will become alienated from you.

- **Encourage them to take small decisions independently.** This will build their self-confidence and give them a sense of independence.

- **Don't talk ill of your children's friends.** Teenagers love their friends very much, and at this age, they are the most important to them. So never talk bad about them or insult them in any way. This will hurt them and alienate them from you.

- **Appreciate their achievements,** even the small ones. When you appreciate even their small achievements, it tells them you believe in their capabilities and motivates them to achieve more.

- **Teenagers may not listen to you,** but they watch you closely and emulate you. Friends, you need to understand that you need to be very careful of how you behave and what you say in front of your children. If you respect your elders, they will do the same. This is how you instil *Sanskaars* into them.

- **Encourage them to exercise and read daily.** Encouraging your teenagers to exercise daily will not only keep them healthy, but will also help them work off the excess energy and keep them calm and centred. Encouraging them to read will broaden their horizons, and it helps them in developing an understanding and adjusting attitude.

Friends, if you bring about these behavioural and thought changes in your life, I guarantee you, you will have an amazing relationship with your teenagers.

Chapter 15

Be The Teenager
That Surprises & Delights
Your Parents

Friends, just as parents need to understand their children's psyche similarly children also have a moral duty to try and understand what would make their parents happy.

My young friends, I am not talking about big earth-shattering changes; I am talking about small behavioural changes and little caring gestures that will keep your parents happy and proud.

- **Wish them good morning and good night daily and hug them and kiss them as you wish them.** As you grow older, I know you feel embarrassed about displays of affection, but darlings, these little gestures of love will make your parents so happy. Just try it, and you will feel the worth of your gesture when you see their happy faces.

- **Try to wake up earlier.** Children usually love to sleep late, and parents want the opposite. Believe me, children, your parents do understand that you have a different sleep cycle than them. However, if you made an effort to wake up a little earlier, it would make them very happy because they worry about all the health issues that can come up due to this, and also they want you to have more time to manage your schedule better.

- **Limit your time on Social Media.** My young friends, your parents give you laptops, tablets and smartphones because they want you to have the best of everything. They want you to be connected to the world and have a top-notch education. Social Media today is an important part of life, but if you limit your time on it and focus on your studies as well.

- **Share about your day with them.** Parents feel happy and connected to you when you share about your life with them. Mothers especially are always super excited to hear what happened at school or college.

- **When you sit down to eat, if something is missing at the table, don't call out to your mother for it.** Instead, get up and fetch it yourself from the kitchen. Your busy mother's heart will swell with pride on seeing this little caring and responsible act.

- **Accompany your parents to family and other functions.** Children often don't want to go to family gatherings or weddings with their parents, they give excuses like we will get bored, there is no one our age etc., but I request you to go with them at least some times if not all the time. It will make them truly happy.

- **Never shout or scream at your parents.** Your parents have brought you into this world; they want only the best for you and are willing to go to any length to give you a happy and comfortable life. You might not always see eye to eye with them, but don't shout at them.

So my young friends, remember your parents are your closest friends and your best well-wishers. Do make these little efforts to make them happy and see them bloom with joy.

Chapter 16

Bonus Tips To Keep Your Relationships Strong

Friends relationships are the true treasures of life, and we should put our heart & soul into maintaining them. In the previous chapters, I have already shared with you how to keep your most important relationships healthy. Here are some more bonus tips.

- Whenever there arises a problem in a relationship, you must work together to find a solution if just one person works at it or dominates it. You will never be able to find common grounds.

- Remember, no one is perfect, including you. There will be many things that your partner will not like about you and vice-a-versa. The key to a beautiful relationship is to focus on the positives and ignore or talk out what you don't like.

- Needs can be fulfilled, but desires are limitless. It may not always be possible to fulfil all of them. Expect less and accept more! Expectation will always lead to disappointment, whereas non-expectation will always surprise you pleasantly.

- The ego is like cancer; it is a silent killer that spells death for relationships. Don't let it control your relationship. Don't hesitate to admit it if you are wrong, and be quick to apologize. It doesn't make you smaller. It shows how much you care about the relationship.

- Friends feeling love is not enough. Expressing it is very important too. Make sure you say I Love You to your partner, children, parents, siblings etc., that you love them every morning and at bedtime. Tell them you trust them, how cherished and respected it will make them feel and when they are away from you, tell them you miss them.

- Friends, it is nice to be important. We all love it when we are made to feel honored or special. But remember, it is even more important to be nice. So make sure that you are always kind, soft spoken and polite to everyone.

- Always remember to say thank you to your family members. Most people take their near and dear ones for granted, but it is important to say please, thank you, and sorry to your parents, partners, children and siblings too. It will make your relationship all the more sweeter.

- Always encourage, appreciate your family members and celebrate their achievements. Tell them how proud you are of them and that you support them completely. Then watch how beautifully they respond to you.

Friends, with all that I have shared with you in this section, I am sure you will improve all your relationships and live a happy and contented life.

YOUR PERSONALITY IS WHO YOU ARE; POLISH THE DIAMOND WITHIN!

Chapter 17

Confidence; The Key To Shining Bright

Confidence is an Inside Job

Confidence is an inside job; it comes from within. It comes from believing in and trusting yourself. Believing that you can handle whatever comes your way.

Friends, in the second section of this book, I have shared the techniques of Mirror Work, Affirmations and connecting to the Universal Power through Meditation. All these will help you believe in yourself. You will feel confident that you are capable of doing anything.

Overcoming fear fosters confidence

Overcoming fear fosters confidence. There are many small and big things that we all fear doing and feel under confident about. Friends start doing those things; step out of your comfort zone. Start by doing the little things; I am not asking you to go Sky Diving or Rapid River Rafting all of a sudden. Take baby steps. If you have never ridden an Uber/Ola alone, overcome your fear and begin now. Take baby steps.

Doing these little things to overcome your fear and step outside your comfort zone will give you huge boosts of confidence.

Do your daily chores yourself

Doing your daily chores yourself is also a confidence booster, friends. Not being dependent on anyone for your daily little chores/needs can be very empowering. Make your own bed, fetch your own water, make your own tea, water the plants, set fresh flowers etc.

Take up a new activity

Friends taking up a new activity or learning something new will empower you, and it will help grow your confidence in leaps & bounds. When you learn or do something new, it activates your brain cells, and you feel more confident and capable. So keep pursuing a new activity or hobby from time to time. It could be anything such as Yoga, Meditation, Zumba, Kick- boxing, and Creative Writing etc.

Walk a little faster

Friends, this may seem like a very simple tip, but it works at a psychological level. Whenever you are walking, consciously try to walk a little faster than your normal pace. Do this regularly and notice the difference in your confidence levels.

Remind yourself of your achievements

Friends, a great way to renew your confidence is to sit down and look back at all that you have achieved. Any time that you have been awarded or applauded, all the times you have been appreciated and think back to all the times you thought you couldn't do something, and you went ahead and did it anyway. This will make you confident immediately.

Help and support others

Make it a point to help and support friends, family and extended family in any way you can physically, emotionally, morally, financially or with your time to the best of your ability. Helping others in this manner boosts your confidence.

Dress it up

While, as I said earlier, confidence is majorly an inside job, there are many things we can do on the outside as well to foster and enhance confidence.

Dressing up well is one of them. When you are well dressed, you feel confident by default. By dressing up I don't mean that you should be wearing only trendy clothes, what I mean is that you should be wearing well-fitted clothes that suit you and that you are comfortable in.

Seal it with a Smile

The biggest confidence booster is your smile. A smile is like a powerhouse that generates megawatts of confidence within you and lights up the world with its radiance. A smile makes approaching anyone easier, and that fills you up with confidence. A genuine smile comes only when you truly love and accept yourself.

Friends with these tips your personality will shine like a diamond, and you will be filled to the brim with confidence.

Chapter **18**

Communication Skills;
Talk Your Way Through Life

The way you communicate speaks a lot about your personality. Your communication is your signature. Make sure you are signing right. There is a common phrase in Hindi that says, ***"Baat karne se hi Baat banti hai"*** broadly translated, it means that only talking it out can solve issues. Communication is such an important part of our careers and relationships.

For our communication to be effective, we must keep certain things in mind and practice them while communicating. Communication is a combination of verbal & non-verbal (body) language. It is important to focus on both.

Verbal Communication
Stay quiet if you have nothing good to say.

Friends, the first rule of good and effective communication is to never be hurtful toward anyone either by your speech or your actions. Constructive criticism is one thing, but being hurtful is completely unacceptable, so if you have nothing good to contribute to the conversation, it's best to stay quiet.

Don't talk politics or religion

While having a conversation with anyone, be it family, friends, work colleagues or even random strangers, it is best not to discuss, comment upon or opine about politics or religion. These topics are ultra-personal, and most people have inflexible views or perspectives about them, which of course, they are entitled to. Since people are very sensitive about these topics, it is advisable to stay away from them to avoid unpleasantness.

Talk energetically and enthusiastically

Whenever you address people or converse with them, you should talk energetically and enthusiastically so that people are interested in talking to you and listening to you. Nobody is interested in communicating with someone who shows no interest or enthusiasm in talking.

Do not interrupt people

A critical rule of good communication is to never interrupt another person before they have completed what they are saying. Talking over people is not only a sign of bad manners; it also shows that you are not paying any attention and have no respect for them.

Don't offer unsolicited advice

Friends, what I am sharing now is one of the most important rules of good communication. Never offer unsolicited advice to anyone. These days everyone is wise enough to make their own decisions. If they need your advice, they will ask for it. You decrease your own worth by offering unsolicited advice and driving people away.

Know what to say when

To be a good communicator, it is important to know what to say, when to say it, and whom to say it. Certain things must only be communicated in private. So it is crucial to talk as per the demands of the situation.

Keep your emotions and voice under control

For communication to be effective, you must stay calm and keep your emotions under control. When you become triggered or angry in any way, your voice will become loud and aggressive, leading to blocked communication.

It's all in the Name

Every person loves to be addressed by their name; their name on another person's lips is music to most people's ears. While talking to people try to address them by name as much as possible. In case they are elder to you address them as sir or ma'am, this will make them feel good or if addressing family address them with appropriate relationship such as *chaachi, maami, nana, jija ji, taya ji* etc.

Non-verbal Communication (Body Language)

Non-verbal clues and body language play an important role in effective communication. Don't forget to pay attention to them while communicating.

Maintain Eye Contact

The most important part of non-verbal communication is eye-contact. While talking to someone, you must look them directly in the eye most of the time. A minimum of 50% eye contact is essential for effective communication. It tells them you are interested in talking to them; it also demonstrates the sincerity and honesty of your intentions while communicating.

Lean In

While talking to a person, if you lean in a little toward them, it shows them that you are listening to them keenly and they have your undivided attention.

Use Hand Gestures

While talking, your communication becomes more effective if you use hand gestures to emphasize or illustrate your point. It makes your conversation interesting and holds the listener captive.

Don't make awkward gestures

Don't make awkward gestures like scratching your head or rubbing your nose, or any other unbecoming gestures while talking to or listening to someone. It is poor manners and leaves the other person feeling awkward too.

Do not keep checking your phone

Friends, it is extremely bad manners to keep looking at your phone while talking to someone. It is disrespectful to them and speaks ill of your personality. If there is something important that you are expecting on your phone or an important call comes in while you are talking, please excuse yourself, seek the other person's permission and then attend to your phone.

Friends, if you follow what I have shared, your communication will be effective all the time, and your career and your relationships will thrive.

Chapter 19

Groom Yourself Right; Impress Everyone!

Friends, developing your confidence and communicating effectively is critical; however, to have an all-around pleasing personality, it is essential to be well presented as well. Your hair, skin, clothes, accessories and styling are essential elements of grooming that you must take care of.

Your Skin speaks before you do

Your personality is the sum total of who you are. When you enter a room, your Skin speaks even before you do. Make sure your skin is healthy and glowing.

In the first two sections of the book, we have discussed the proper diet, exercise and lifestyle, which will contribute greatly to healthy glowing skin.

Sharing a few tips here with you to maintain your Skin and let its radiance outshine your diamonds.

- Stay hydrated; drink at least 8 glasses of water a day. Don't just gulp the water; take small sips.

- After washing your face with an appropriate Face Wash in the morning, follow it up with a Moisturizer and Sunscreen Lotion. Use Sunscreen even if you are staying inside the house. Sun rays can reach inside as well.

- Only use good quality products, cosmetics and makeup on your skin. Don't compromise on skin health.

- Do not ever go to bed with your makeup on. Cleanse and wash your face at bedtime, apply a moisturizer or night cream before going to bed. I recommend using Almond oil on your face and neck. It works wonders for the Skin.

- Hair, Nails & Lips can truly seal the deal

Hair & Now!

Hair is as important as what you wear. No matter how good your clothes are, it will all go to waste if your hair is unkempt. So are your nails. Chipped nails and chapped lips are a complete no.

- Your hair should always be clean, washed and combed well.

- Oil your hair at least once a week. It will keep your hair healthy. I recommend Onion Hair oil. Nowadays it is readily available from many good brands.

- You are free to choose and sport whatever haircut or hairstyle appeals to you but keep it well.

- Style your hair as per the environment and occasion. Keep it simple, sleek and stylish at the workplace. Experiment with it outside work if you so want.

- If ever in a dilemma about what hairstyling is best as you have multiple events to go to, I recommend styling it straight. Straight hair works on all outfits and in all situations.

Nailing It!

- Keep your nails well filed and clean.

- If you can't keep your nails clean, clip them short. Unclean nails are unhygienic and look ugly.

- If you wear nail polish, make sure it's well-kept and smooth.

- Chipped nail polish looks shabby and reflects poorly on your personality.

- Go for neutral colors at work.

- Lucky Lips!

- Chapped and dry lips look ugly and are a sign of your careless attitude toward self-care.

- Use Lip-balm frequently throughout the day to keep your lips soft & smooth.

- When wearing Lip Color, make sure your Lip line is clean and check that your teeth are not smudged.

Fitted to the T

Your Outfit is an integral part of your personality. Make sure it speaks volumes.

- Having a great outfit doesn't necessarily mean it has to be expensive or from a big brand.

- Always wear a well-fitted outfit, neither too loose nor too tight. Too loose, and you will look like a sack, too tight-you won't be able to move comfortably. So find the balance, don't blindly follow fashions & trends.

- Your clothes should always be clean and well ironed.

- Balance is important. Do not wear too many colours or prints together. If wearing a loosely fitted top, pair it with a fitted trouser/skirt and vice-a-versa. Pair Loose bottoms with fitted tops.

- Avoid wearing short tops with leggings and jeggings.

- Try to wear trousers or palazzos that are ankle-length; this length will make you look stylish and smart.

- Always have the classic black and white shirts/Indian suits in your wardrobe. These are colors you can never go wrong with and are easy to accessorize.

Style it like a Pro

Once your hair & outfit are in place, it is vital to add some spice to your personality by styling yourself up a bit.

- There is a universe of exciting and attractive earrings available these days. Amp up your look with a pair of unique earrings, and watch your look go from good to great.

- Belt it up. Accentuating loose dresses with stylish belts is a great styling secret. Use it to stand out from the crowd.

- Use scarves to make a stylish statement. Scarves are available in a lot of styles, materials and colors. Make abundant use of them.

- To complete your look, wear Bellies or Peep Toes (either flat or heeled). It finishes your look beautifully. In winters complete your look with a pair of stylish yet comfortable boots (Ankle-length, Mid-calf, Knee-length or Thigh-high)

- Do not wear a bracelet or a bangle(s) along with your watch. Let your watch make the statement if you want to wear bangles/ bracelets etc., wear them on the other hand.

Don't just look good; smell good too

To make a great impression, this is perhaps the most crucial part of grooming. No matter how good you look, if you smell foul, it all goes to waste.

- Use deodorant and perfume to mitigate body odour and smell pleasant.

- Sometimes, people wear clothes straight out of the closet without airing them or wear their clothes too many times before washing/dry cleaning them. Such clothes smell bad, don't make this mistake. Not even perfume can take care of this.

- Ensure that you wear washed/dry cleaned clothes only and give your clothes sufficient time to air to get the stale smell out if they have been stored too long.

- Just as body odour is a big put-off, so is mouth/breath odour. Brush your teeth twice a day. Gargle with mouthwash before going out and use a mouth freshener such as **Elaichi** (Cardamom) to keep your breath smelling pleasant.

Friends, the grooming tips I have shared in this chapter will definitely help you make a terrific impression on people.

Chapter 20

Bonus Tips To Shine
Like A Diamond

In this chapter, I am sharing some priceless bonus tips with you in addition to the gems I have already shared earlier on the various topics.

The most important thing about your personality is your attitude; however well you may be dressed and accessorized, it is of no worth unless you have the right attitude toward life, work and people.

- The first rule to having a great personality and attitude is always to wear a great smile. A smiling face is like a magnet. It attracts and impresses everyone. It tells people that you are a warm and welcoming person.

- Be open-minded and change along with the changing times. In today's times' values and morals have shifted as they often do with time. While sticking to fundamental human values, it is also essential to change to new ways of thinking. If you are rigid and keep sticking to outdated principles, people will not want to interact with you.

- Another excellent personality trait is to talk less about yourself and ask more about the person you are talking to. Try to find out what their interests and opinions are and tailor your conversation accordingly. People will be drawn to you by this trait.

- Respecting people and valuing human dignity is a personality trait that will always make you loved and admired by many. Friends, it's essential to respect each individual and treat them with dignity irrespective of their age, gender, or socioeconomic status.

- Be appreciative and encouraging toward people. Compliment them genuinely. Do not give fake compliments just to please people. However, if you genuinely appreciate people, you will form a long-lasting bond with them.

- Be kind, courteous and well mannered always; being rich and beautiful is no good if you are not well mannered or well behaved. Your true worth and value are visible in how you treat those who serve you, such as Coolies, Waiters, Domestic Support Staff, Cleaners, Janitors, Guards & Peons, etc.

- Friends, another valuable tip is not to be available for everyone always. I don't mean you should not be there for people; what I mean is don't let people take you for granted. Prioritize and value yourself.

- My dear friends never have a defeatist attitude. Always give your 100% to everything. Remember, Luck can be changed with Hard Work. Optimism and sincerity are great personality traits.

- Be happy with what you have; if you are not satisfied with it, work toward achieving what you want. Do not keep complaining about lack. Nobody likes a complaining and negative attitude.

- Another great tip to keep your personality upbeat is never to lounge around in your night clothes the whole day. Even if you don't have to go to work or out of the house, get dressed. It will instantly make you feel alive and energetic.

- Routine often becomes boring, so hair is a great way to break the monotony of your external personality. Keep changing and experimenting with new haircuts and styles to give a new edge to your personality.

Friends, I have shared with you everything I believe in and practice to make my life wonderful. I hope you will incorporate these into your life and take it to the happiest level.

Do not let this book be the end of our connection and conversation. **Connect with me on my YouTube Channel Poonam Kalra 60,** where I will continue to share new ways of living our best life. Here's the link to my YouTube channel https://youtube.com/channel/UCN-jbt5PFJHIzFcIl5MxjLg

Also, you can call upon me to connect with you all and motivate you. I'd be delighted to address you and to celebrate life together. Connect with me by visiting my website www.poonamklra.com

Friends, you may also connect with me through Facebook & Instagram.

https://www.facebook.com/poonam.kalra.961

https://www.instagram.com/poonam.kalra.961/